The Wellspring Crew

Navigator Series 1

Real-Life Stories of Leaders and How They Built Their Brand

Illustrated by Nicola Anderson.

ISBN: 978-1-7323638-0-9

DEDICATION

To all the learners out there who ask big questions.

TABLE OF CONTENTS

INTRODUCTION

Dear Reader...

We are so excited to have you embark on the first installment of The Navigator Series, brought to you by The Wellspring Crew. The Wellspring Crew is a collection of accomplished adults (we refer to them as our "Crew") who have found achievement in the real world and who desire to use that success as a platform to inform and inspire you! We want you, as a young reader, to know how to use your dreams and desires to impact your world.

This book is designed for you: a curious reader who asks curious questions. Our conversations with our Crew Contributors are focused around the ideas that are the foundation of an educational program we would like to share with you. 7 Mindsets is an organization that teaches students that they are responsible for their happiness and success. The 7 Mindsets are:

1. Everything Is Possible
2. Passion First
3. We Are Connected
4. 100% Accountable
5. Attitude of Gratitude
6. Live to Give
7. The Time Is Now

Our leaders experienced all of these mindsets in their stories. And just like you, the best leaders have moments of mistakes, failures, challenges, joys, and accomplishments. They didn't just wake up one day as "the boss." Along the journey to becoming a boss, the leaders profiled in this book learned about the importance of confidence, hard work, gratefulness, the value of relationships, and successful teamwork.

We desire for this book to be read alongside an adult in your life, as we hope this will spark further questions, conversations, and ideas.

In the first edition of the Navigator Series we are discussing leaders who have created a brand. What is a brand?

> # brand
> /brand/
>
> *noun*
>
> 1. a type of product manufactured by a particular company under a particular name.
>   "a new brand of detergent"

A brand is a name, term, design, symbol, or other feature that distinguishes an organization or product from its **competitors**. A defined brand creates individuality and uniqueness among companies.

In the stories we share our featured leaders have created a whole variety of brands. These brands include Muse Hair Salon, fab'rik (a clothing boutique), King of Pops (a popsicle empire), Dutch Monkey Doughnuts (a gourmet doughnut shop), and Lighthouse Family Retreat (a charitable organization). Brands can come in all shapes and sizes. The product behind each brand is different, but they all share common goals: to be unique in the marketplace, have a quality product or service, and then also find a way to give back to others.

After reading these stories, we hope that you will find a new or increased desire to make a mark on your world and that you will be inspired to work hard, play hard, and enjoy all the discoveries that life has in store for you.

Happy reading!

CHAPTER 1
DANIEL MASON JONES

Be Confident

Many years ago, a little boy named Daniel grew up in a loving and accepting family in a small town in South Carolina. Like many people in small towns, he lived a simple childhood, but Daniel's **community** was very different than most. His community was strict and had strong beliefs that didn't allow for many things that seem common to others. For example, women could not cut their hair or wear pants, and children were never allowed to watch TV. Yes, you read that correctly: They *never* watched TV. Although for most people this would seem like an impossible way of life, Daniel really didn't feel like he missed out. Now that he is older, he thinks that this allowed for him to develop an extra creative mind that would eventually serve him quite well.

Throughout Daniel's childhood quite a few challenges tested his ability to face difficulty head-on. When he was younger he was bullied—because people thought he was different. But aren't we all different? He remembers thinking that his friends had all sorts of talents in sports and in schoolwork, but he didn't see the talents that he had. He felt like he was a misfit. In middle school, Daniel would not each lunch in the lunchroom because he didn't want to get teased. Instead of spending money on lunch, he saved up his money to purchase flowers that he planted at a retirement home. Daniel remembers the great feeling of joy and pride knowing that, although he was feeling kind of crummy, he was able to make a great impact on the residents of the retirement home.

THINK BIG

Even as a student, you can bring joy to those around you (like Daniel did with the residents of the retirement home). What are some ways you can do something you love that also has a positive impact on those around you?

Although Daniel experienced the challenges of being teased and feeling like he did not fit in, he had a creative mind that would dream about what life may look like outside of his community. When he was in eighth grade, Daniel drew a picture in art class of a very detailed image of a home. When Daniel was much older, his dad told him to pull out that picture from a box full of old schoolwork. When he did so, Daniel realized that the house he lived in was the house he drew when he was younger. Daniel believes that the ability to **visualize** certain goals and dreams can later turn them into reality.

THINK BIG

What are some life events you visualize for your future?

While growing up, Daniel didn't have too many dreams and goals about the type of career he wanted. But in high school, he became fascinated with the funeral business and thought it would be interesting to become a funeral director. This is the person that is responsible for managing all the details of a funeral service for someone who has passed away. A funeral director is probably not the most common job of interest to high schoolers, but this is what makes Daniel so unique: He is true to himself and what he is passionate about.

After graduating from high school, Daniel set off to college in Atlanta to become a funeral director. Daniel completed his studies and, upon graduation, was offered a job at a funeral home. One day at work he was prepping for a funeral service and the hairstylist scheduled to work that day didn't show up. Daniel stepped in and he fell in love with working on hair. A new passion was born! Daniel then realized that he didn't want to work in the funeral business. Instead, he wanted to work in the salon business. So, back to school he went!

As a graduate of the salon program, he was once again ready for real-world work experience. This time around, Daniel was hooked. He felt like this was where he belonged. Quickly after graduating from salon school, Daniel found success and happiness serving his clients. As a child he felt like he didn't have any talents. But as a hairstylist he has shown tremendous talents in his ability to serve so many types of clients and their unique hair needs. Daniel has not only been a talented hairstylist, but he has also become a talented leader and educator. Daniel created a side business where he travels around the country educating other hairstylists about how to build their own businesses.

Today, as the owner and creative director of his own salon, Muse Salon and Spa, Daniel has found great joy and accomplishment in serving his clients, mentoring new employees, and giving back to his community. His favorite part of being a leader is building relationships with people. Both clients and staff look up to him and appreciate his ideas. As a business owner, Daniel feels that he has been given so much that it is his job to also serve his community. He is so passionate about serving foundations that provide funds for children with cancer that every September his salon picks one special day where they donate all of the proceeds to cancer research.

THINK BIG

If you could pick a charity to donate to, what organization would you choose?

Daniel's story is a great example of a young boy who had small dreams but felt like he didn't have a lot to offer to the world. As he grew up Daniel remained focused on learning and his studies. That path brought Daniel to where he is today: an incredibly accomplished professional who gives back to others is so many ways. If you were to meet Daniel, he would tell you that you are perfect just the way you are. Be true to yourself, study hard, listen to the adults around you, and find your passions.

THINK BIG

How can you show confidence in being who you are?

BRAND SPOTLIGHT: MUSE SALON AND SPA

Muse salonandspa

Service: Everything you need for the ultimate salon and spa experience—creative excellence, unparalleled hospitality, cutting-edge technology, and a passionate team that is highly trained and extremely talented.

Why did they name their business "Muse"? A muse is source of inspiration for a creative person. Each and every stylist at their salon has a unique source of inspiration.

For more information about Muse, please visit:
www.musesalonandspa.com.

YOUR THOUGHTS AND IDEAS AFTER READING DANIEL'S STORY

CHAPTER 2
DANA SPINOLA

Trust Your Gut

If you combined a fierce, competitive athlete with a fashion-loving, heel-wearing stylist, what would you get? The answer is Dana Spinola! Dana is the founder of fab'rik, a boutique whose mission is "High Fashion with Heart." Dana completely embodies that mission. Dana's story is one that displays a driven sense to always succeed and do good at the same time. But not all is a winning game in the journey to success.

Dana grew up in a loving and passion-focused family. Her dad was an artist and her mom was an interior designer. They completely displayed a life in which you do what you love. Unfortunately, sometimes the pursuit of a passion-filled profession still has challenges. Although her parents loved their work in the art industries, they didn't have a lot of financial freedom. As a way to save money for the family, Dana's mom made all of her clothes. Dana loved this because she felt like she had her own personal designer and stylist. It was clear that fashion was in Dana's heart at a very early age, but she didn't have any idea how to turn it into a profession.

It is also important to note that even though she was a fashion-loving girl, she was also an extremely fierce competitor. Dana played soccer and basketball, and she was a competitive runner. Many teachers and coaches spotted in Dana the natural ability to lead. She had zero fear, and the same skill that allowed her to win a race also served her well in the future.

When Dana attended college, there wasn't an opportunity to study fashion. Early on, Dana knew she wanted to excel in the professional world and have a life that didn't include stress over finances. Dana met with her school counselor and discussed various majors. The counselor encouraged her to pursue a degree in management information systems, a course of study that focuses on business skills and technology. Upon graduation from college, Dana was offered a job with a well-known company. She traveled all over the nation as a consultant. Her job was very challenging and rewarding at the same time. She was excelling quite quickly within this role, but after a few years, Dana started to feel that her end goal would not be manageable if she continued on this path. Dana always knew that she wanted to be a mom and have a successful career, but she felt like the amount of traveling required for her job didn't match her personal long-term goal.

After this realization, Dana left her consulting job and took a job in Atlanta. She worked during the day and spent her evenings working on her **business plan**. She also took a job working at a boutique on the weekends. This second job was a very important choice that helped Dana experience the real-world highs and lows of working in a boutique. Sure, she loved being around clothes, but could she handle walking in heels all day long?!

At that time in her life, Dana was experiencing the intersection of passion and purpose. Dana describes passion as identifying "What do you love?" and passion as "What does the world need?" When those two worlds combine you have found your sweet spot!

In 2002, after one year of planning and preparing, Dana successfully accomplished her dream of opening her very own boutique. Dana explains her happiness on that first day of opening fab'rik like being awake in a dream. This was the highest of high moments for her. She had a fashion show and amazing sales, and all of her friends and family were there to support her opening. However, that intense high was short lived, because the *very* next morning when Dana opened the store, she realized her store had been broken into. *Everything* had been stolen. The first person she called was her

dad, and his response was "Welcome to owning your own business." Dana felt so much anger, frustration, and sadness that day. But she would not let that stop her. She called all of her **vendors** to order more clothes, and she was quickly ready to re-open.

THINK BIG

Time to problem-solve: How would you handle the situation of having your brand-new store getting damaged and robbed?

Soon after her first store re-opened, customers requested that Dana open another location. After opening the second store, Dana heard more and more requests for other locations, including requests from other states. Dana had planned to have one—maybe two—locations, but expanding into other states was not a part of her desire. As more and more women approached her, Dana had a new idea: Maybe she could help other women like herself leave their corporate jobs and have the same impact in their own communities. This was the launch of the **franchise** side of Dana's business, and she sees this growth as the opportunity to expand her mission. Meaning that her business could spread their mission, "High Fashion with Heart" to cities all over our country and Dana would not have to travel as she did earlier in her career.

THINK BIG

How can you, as a student, "expand your mission"? How can you inspire others with what you find interesting and exciting?

As the business grew and grew, a new undertaking was placed on Dana's heart. The company had donated clothes to local organizations, but Dana was thinking that they could go above and beyond in the spirit of giving. What if she was able to combine that same love of styling a customer to help girls and women in need? Dana founded her charitable organization, Free fab'rik, whose mission is to remind girls and women that they are beautiful and worthy. These customers truly feel transformed by the experience of being dressed by professionals. Dana and her team believe they are greatly changing lives by changing the outward "armor" of these women.

Throughout her life Dana has had mentors and leaders who have impacted her in so many different ways. When Dana was in ninth grade, a math teacher told her that she should go into the Air Force. That probably would not have been the best profession for her, as Dana is terrified of heights, but her teacher told her that she was remarkable and could do anything. Taking to heart those positive affirmations that others share with us is a great lesson. As an adult, Dana has found mentors who embody a skill or talent that she is seeking to better. She met one mentor after a chance encounter when Dana's daughter was petting a woman's dog. Dana later learned this woman was a highly influential leader of a women's group, and Dana boldly asked if they could meet and chat because Dana valued her leadership of women and she desired to further her ability to be a positive leader. People come into our lives for all different reasons, and it is our responsibility to identify which moments will allow us to grow and become the best version of ourselves.

THINK BIG

What positive statements are you hearing from those around you?

Now that Dana has successfully launched and grown a business, she sees herself as someone who needs to pay it forward and mentor others. Whether it is a chat with a teammate to give advice or participating on an **advisory board** for boutique owners, Dana believes that finding a mentor and then becoming one is so important to allow others to make bold choices and find growth. But as a successful business owner, it becomes increasingly difficult to meet all

of the needs of people around her. For Dana, the hardest part of being a business leader is knowing that there are times when she has to say "no." A great leader is one that shows courage to say no- even when the invitation sounds so exciting.

THINK BIG

Who would you put on your advisory board? Who are the people around you that you can learn from?

THINK BIG

When have you had to show courage to say "no"? Perhaps you received an invitation to play with a friend but you had homework to finish. Can you think of examples in your life?

On the other hand, there are also great feelings that come from being a leader. Dana's favorite part of being a business leader is to see the influence her business has on her customers. She loves to be a part of a customer coming in to get dressed up for a special occasion. She had a very special memory of wearing a simple $19 dress on the opening night of her store. She felt bold and beautiful in that dress, which now hangs in her home office as a reminder of moment. Dana loves being a part of these special moments for women.

Dana's journey as a young competitor to a successful business owner displays all of the high and lows that make up the greatest of stories: lessons learned, relationships formed, and goals accomplished. Trusting your gut is the biggest lesson Dana wants to share with others. Someone once told Dana that an idea comes into your mind, travels down to your heart, and ends up in your gut. Even if your gut leads you into a hard lesson, find the growth in both the good and the bad experiences, because you have one life to live. That makes your story perfectly imperfect!

BRAND SPOTLIGHT: FAB'RIK

Vision: To create boutiques where everyone can afford to feel beautiful.

Mission: High style with heart, no attitude or sticker shock.

In the news: An article in *Entrepreneur* magazine listed fab'rik as a top 500 franchise

For more information about fab'rik, please visit: www.fabrikstyle.com.

YOUR THOUGHTS AND IDEAS AFTER READING DANA'S STORY

Create Unexpected Moments of Happiness

What special treat do you enjoy now that one day you think you could make a business out of? Yes, it is actually possible to make a business out of that special treat that you love! Several years ago a little boy named Steven was busy dreaming up a life as a future soccer player. Little did he know that one day he would go on to build a popsicle empire. King of Pops was built after an unfortunate job loss, but sometimes a loss can turn in to a blessing—when you are open to a challenge.

Steven grew up in a loving family with two older brothers, and he spent much of his childhood playing any and all sports. He didn't think too much about a job in the real world, because he thought he could just play soccer forever. However, he must have had some natural business skills. When Steven was younger his mom had Steven and his brothers create a **budget** for their expenses. Because he was a 10-year-old, Steven's budget displayed the spending money allowances his parents would financially support. His budget included items like haircuts and fun spending money. While out shopping one day he saw that a pair of hair clippers that cost $20. Although that was twice the amount he had budgeted, Steven knew that if he cut his own hair he could still get the allowance for haircuts and then save that money for something else later. Steven often looked for ways to be **financially responsible**.

What would your budget look like? What are ways you could earn money?

As a student he showed an early interest in **entrepreneurship.** One business he started in high school was created after playing disc golf with friends. Disc golf is played on a golf course, but, instead of clubs and golf balls, you throw a frisbee toward the hole. The course where Steven and his friends played had a small lake—in which many people lost their frisbees. Steven thought that if he fished for the frisbees after playing disc golf, he could then sell the frisbees online. Right then was the start of a very interesting new business!

When Steven realized a career as a frisbee fisherman wasn't in the cards, he knew that college was the best choice to pursue his next interest: writing. After high school Steven studied journalism at the University of Georgia. He dreamed about becoming a journalist, following all of the most interesting stories, and then writing about them for other people. When he graduated from college he took a job as a journalist for a newspaper in Jackson, Wyoming. He quickly fell in love with all of the fun activities in Wyoming, especially skiing, but Steven soon realized that his hobbies were becoming more expensive than he could afford. He thought about changing his career path, and his older brother suggested Steven come back to Georgia and take a position at the same insurance company where his brother worked. In this position Steven worked as a product analyst. That means Steven studied and investigated all sorts of **data** within the insurance company. He then used the information he discovered to make suggestions for customers based upon what he found. While he enjoyed analyzing information, he was disappointed that he never got to see if his work was providing a positive benefit to the customers. At the time that Steven was working at this insurance company, our nation's **economy**

was going through a very challenging time. Steven saw many co-workers lose their jobs, so he knew he needed to start thinking about what he would do if he too lost his job. Just as he was planning for the possibility, Steven did end up losing his job, giving him the chance to embark on a new adventure.

At this time in Steven's life he spent a great amount of time traveling with his other brother around Central America and Mexico. During their travels they enjoyed a common treat in every country called a paleta, similar to what we call popsicles in the U.S. Paletas are usually a unique flavor and always sold in the street by a cart vendor. After many travels and countless paletas, Steven and his brother Nick decided to bring this concept to Atlanta. As Steven was now in full-force planning for the new business, Nick decided he too was ready for an adven-

THINK BIG

What challenge are you going through that could actually be seen as an opportunity?

ture. He left his career in the legal field and joined forces with Steven. This was the beginning of the King of Pops!

King of Pops has become an icon to the festival, community, and outside-entertainment culture in the southeastern United States—but it certainly didn't happen overnight. Plans were changed, challenges needed to be faced, and relationships needed to be built. It has been a long but positive road. In the early planning days, Steven envisioned King of Pops being a store, like an ice cream store, but starting a store required more money than Steven had available. Then Steven had another idea: In Central America, paletas are sold by push carts, so he decided to sell from a push cart, too. Then there were challenges with what the law allowed. Local laws control what vendors can sell and where they can sell their goods.

Because King of Pops has been so successful with this type of business, they now work with the local government to help create and design the laws that are best for everyone.

They also had challenges with flavors. When King of Pops started to sell their products, they sold unique and special flavors, like pineapple habanero, tamarind mango chili, and tangerine basil (like they do in Central America and Mexico). These were interesting, but people were asking for simple flavors like chocolate and strawberry. Steven learned that people like to see special flavors, but they also want to see some flavors that they are familiar with. All new businesses encounter some type of challenge, but Steven was able to face each situation, learn from it, and move on as he improved his business.

Remember earlier in our story when Steven felt discouraged in his position at the insurance company because he didn't know if his work was creating a positive impact? While Steven built his own brand, it was important for Steven to see the benefit of his product. King of Pops' greatest desire is to create "Unexpected Moments of Happiness" for their customers. You know that feeling, when you open a sweet treat, take that first bite and then a smile overtakes your face? King of Pops has allowed for Steven to serve his customers directly and immediately see the impact of his hard work. These are the unexpected moments of happiness.

THINK BIG

"Unexpected Moments of Happiness" don't only come from eating a popsicle. How can you be a part of unexpected moments of happiness for those around you?

Now that King of Pops has been around for almost eight years, they have had the opportunity to expand the business into new areas and reach an even larger audience. One of the new businesses that has come out of King of Pops is King of Crops. They purchased a farm in Georgia, with the goal to provide locally sourced produce to use in the production of their popsicles. "From crop to pop" is what they say!

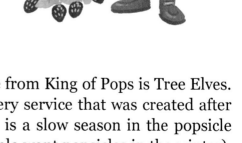

When the conversation of passion comes into play, it is super important to Steven that he creates businesses that not only talk about being good to nature, but that are truly stewards to the land. This means that so many aspects of Steven's businesses will leave nature better off in the long run because of his business.

Another unique business that has come from King of Pops is Tree Elves. This business is a Christmas tree delivery service that was created after the realization that, even though there is a slow season in the popsicle business (apparently not too many people want popsicles in the winter), an opportunity could be found in what seemed like a challenge.

There are so many interesting examples that display Steven as a leader who has dreamed big, focused on a goal, and maintained the desire to be an honorable land preserver. He knows he has been blessed with an idea, timing, and a great product, but above all else, Steven is grateful for all that he gets to be a part of.

And in case you were wondering, Steven's favorite popsicle flavor is Banana Puddin'!

BRAND SPOTLIGHT: KING OF POPS

Product and Goal: Their first priority is to make a great product: the popsicle! They made 2.2 million pops last year!

In their facility they can make up to 10,000 pops in one day! Their pop carts may look small but they can hold up to 600 tasty pops.

They have made close to 500 flavors over the years.

Most popular flavors: Banana Puddin', Peach, Blackberry Ginger Lemonade, and Chocolate Sea Salt

For more information about King of Pops, please visit: www.kingofpops.com.

YOUR THOUGHTS AND IDEAS AFTER READING STEVEN'S STORY

CHAPTER 4
ARPANA SATYU-BURGE

All Relationships Matter

If you were to write in your yearbook what you want to be when you grow up, what would you write? Arpana was interested in so many future jobs that she mentioned them all in her yearbook. Now as an adult, one particular job has led her to be a local business leader. Arpana and her husband are the owners of a specialty doughnut shop. Her story highlights a girl who faced family pressure to measure up, personal health challenges, and the simplistic desire to make a quality product that others will enjoy.

Growing up in a family of business owners outside of Dallas, Texas, Arpana commonly helped out with the family businesses on weekends. She saw her parents enjoy their jobs, and this instilled in her an early love for working. It wasn't always glamourous or fun, but it was a lifelong lesson to see that her mom loved to be a dance teacher and own her own dance school and her dad loved to be a doctor. Arpana also had incredibly influential relationships with her grandma and great-grandma who lived in India while she was growing up. These amazingly accomplished women worked in all sorts of leadership positions. Her great-grandma owned a sari shop. (Saris are beautiful and ornate dresses traditionally worn by women in India.) Arpana's grandma started a college for women in India as well as an orphanage that educates and trains young girls with skills so that they can also grow up to be accomplished leaders in the workplace. It is safe to say that early on Arpana was surrounded by female leaders who made a tremendous impact on their surroundings—and on Arpana.

As a young student, Arpana often dreamed about what her future may look like, but the specifics of that dream often changed. She thought about being a doctor, or a dancer, or a lawyer. Whatever she picked she knew that she wanted to have fun in her job. After graduating high school, she went on to college at Columbia University in New York City. Arpana found it quite difficult to pick a major. She started off studying physics but then changed her course of study to architecture and Eastern religions. Arpana very much enjoyed studying architecture, but she quickly learned that a profession with that degree would mean that she would mostly be working at a computer, and that just wasn't what she wanted to do for the rest of her life.

About the time when Arpana was trying to figure out her course of study, she had a breakdown at school. She was experiencing a very stressful situation and she did not know how to best handle it on her own. The school suggested that she take some time off from Columbia. She went home to Texas to study until she later returned to New York. It would take Arpana many years to fully understand why she had a breakdown, but for the time being she was trying to focus on her studies. Arpana soon realized that traditional college was not for her. She loved to study, but when it came to what she loved to learn, the professional life did not match up with the desires of how she wanted to live her life. She decided she needed to leave school for good—or at least *this* type of school.

THINK BIG

Live to learn! Not everything you like to study has to turn into a job. What are some things you simply like to study?

A young person not attending school must have some kind of idea of what work you can do so that you can afford your rent and groceries. Arpana made a list of all of her interests and strengths to discover some ideas that could allow her to make a living. She liked to travel, so could she be a travel agent? No, she didn't want to be a travel agent. She was quite flexible, so how about joining the circus as a contortionist? Yes! That sounded like a great plan! Arpana looked up when the circus was coming to town, and she had one month of time she needed to fill with another activity before she could run off and join the circus. Arpana's sis-

ter suggested she take a baking class. Arpana liked to bake and cook, so she thought it would be a fun, short-lived class where she could pick up some useful skills while she waited for the circus to come to town.

However, Arpana's plan quickly changed when she fell in love with her baking course! So long, circus—Arpana is going to be a baker! During Arpana's time as a culinary school student, she was given an opportunity to have an **internship** at a well-known and respected restaurant of the highly successful chef Bobby Flay. During the day she attended classes, and in the evenings Arpana worked as a pastry chef intern. Her time under Bobby Flay's guidance not only improved her culinary skills, but she also remembers that he was an amazing leader who looked out for everyone, even the interns. Arpana really appreciated having a leader who asked about her family and encouraged her to grow and improve her skills.

THINK BIG

Is there a business you think is interesting and you would one day want to do an internship with?

One night the pastry chef who was to work on duty alongside Arpana did not show up. This was Arpana's call to step up and show her ability to perform as a paid employee. This moment launched her career as a pastry chef. It is typical in the New York restaurant world to start your career at one location for one year before going to another location. This job movement allows for culinary professionals to gain new experiences and styles from other restaurants. Not all experiences were the same as working for Bobby Flay. Arpana remembers some bosses that were terrible to work for. One boss even stole her recipe book!

At one new location, what started out as a working relationship between two chefs did not stay that way for long. Arpana now refers to that chef as her husband, Martin. Soon after their daughter was born, Arpana and Martin moved to Atlanta to be closer to Martin's family. They both found successful jobs in Atlanta's culinary businesses, but their schedules always crossed, and they never seemed to see each other. They knew they needed to make another change.

This time, they experienced a different type of birth together: the birth of their new business, Dutch Monkey Doughnuts. The idea of a doughnut shop actually had been in the back of Arpana's mind for a while. In New York City, she had thought a doughnut truck at a subway stop would be a huge hit. Now she got to tweak and test out that idea in Georgia. Telling friends and family that they wanted to leave their successful careers within the restaurant business to start a doughnut shop was not always well received by Arpana and Martin's friends and family. Many thought they were, well, crazy. But they were not! Arpana and Martin researched, studied, and planned so much that

they knew this would be a successful business venture. Before they even started construction on their shop, Arpana studied the traffic patterns around them. She sat, watched, and literally counted the cars that passed by her street corner to make sure that there was plenty of existing traffic. She studied, read, and taught herself about running your own business. She had not taken typical business classes in school, so she read all sorts of books about how to start a business. And she planned a very detailed and thorough schedule. She determined an opening date and plotted all of the target dates and goals that needed to be accomplished prior to the grand opening.

One important detail about opening your own business is to determine how you are going to pay for all the expenses. To open the doughnut shop, Arpana needed to purchase baking equipment, chairs and tables, a counter to display product, and so many more items. In order to help fund for these purchases she sold her minivan and got a **loan** from her family.

Deciding to open a business is one challenge that Arpana and her husband were focused and dedicated to tackling on their own. Another ongoing challenge that had traveled along her journey with her was her challenge with a sickness called bipolar disorder. Arpana was not diagnosed with this until she was an adult, but now she can see instances of the sickness when she was younger. Remember when it was suggested that she take a break from college? She thinks she was experiencing a period of challenge with bipolar disorder at that time. Although it is never fun to get a diagnosis, Arapana feels empowered to now have a "map" that she can use to help her during these challenges. For Arpana, and for most people, it is important to always make sure you are confident to talk to people around you when you are experiencing a difficult time. She feels that this is only a bump in the road and that this shows much more resilience than a problem.

THINK BIG
If you are going through a challenging time, who can you talk to about it?

Now that Arpana has been a successful small business owner for more than 10 years, she has learned that there are great parts to being a leader and there are challenges as well. She loves getting to know her customers, for example. When she was a pastry chef at restaurants she never was able to spend time with her customers. Some of Arpana's great friends

today started out as her customers! Arpana also enjoys being a leader that chooses to give back as well. Dutch Monkey hosted a charity event where she had her hair shaved off in support of cancer research. On the other hand, there are some challenges when you are the boss. Managing people can be really hard. When you own your own business, you need to be able to handle all kinds of personalities and problems. If a worker doesn't show up, the owner needs to step in and fill in that spot.

THINK BIG

What are some fun and creative doughnut flavors you would want to create?

At the end of the day, Arpana and Martin are so proud of the brand they have built and the impact they have on their community. They are focused on producing a quality product that their customers will always rave about. Their journey displays the dynamic relationships on their path and the ability to focus on their "map" but at the same time also being flexible to new adventures that can come along the way!

BRAND SPOTLIGHT:
DUTCH MONKEY DOUGHNUTS

Product and Process: No mixes, no buckets of pre-made fillings or icings. No preservatives or stabilizers. Doughnuts the way doughnuts should be made.

They named their business after their daughter's nickname "Monkey" and the trivia fact that doughnuts were introduced to America by the Dutch.

In one year they use approximately 18,000 pounds of sugar. One very special ingredient allows for their yeast doughnuts to have a unique and special flavor and texture- potatoes!

For more information about Dutch Monkey Doughnuts, please visit: www.dutchmonkeydoughnuts.com.

YOUR THOUGHTS AND IDEAS AFTER READING ARPANA'S STORY

CHAPTER 5
CHRIS WOODRUFF

Think About Others First

After experiencing a childhood of fun and mischief, it's hard to imagine what may come as an adult. For Chris Woodruff, the story of growth, learning, and leadership has landed him the in his current position as the CEO of Lighthouse Family Retreat. Chris started out as a young man who was living life with little purpose, but he has certainly grown to become a highly successful business leader who has found great value in serving others.

Most of Chris's childhood in Atlanta was focused around anything and everything athletics related. In fact, you could say that athletics distracted him from excelling at academics or pursing other interests. He had few dreams about a future career, or even going to college. Midway through high school he decided to stop swimming so that he could have more social time with his friends. As an adult, he feels like that choice was probably not the wisest choice to make, but his priority at that time was all about having fun.

THINK BIG

Athletics are a great addition to the experience of growing up. What benefits can athletics bring to students?

After high school Chris enrolled in a community college, where his trend of unfocused studies continued. Things quickly took a turn during a summer job after his first year of college. His summertime job was at a factory that made the foam tomahawks for the Atlanta Braves. During his time at this job he met an older factory worker, a great guy who taught Chris so much about working in a real job. One thing that he didn't intend to teach Chris was that a life as a factory work was really hard. It was hard to make sure you could pay your bills, it was hard to feel that this was living your dream job, and it was hard to think about any future accomplishments. Due to his relationship with his working friend, Chris started to realize that if he didn't get his act together, he would end up with a career just like this older man. This was the first moment when Chris intentionally stopped to think: "What am I do-ing with my life?" He'd been given advice to stop and look back at the choices he'd made, because those choic-es got him to where he was. After thinking about it, Chris decided to totally change the direction that his path was going.

When he returned to school, Chris realized that one of his main challeng-es was that he had never learned *how* to be a student. He didn't have the proper **study skills** needed to become a successful student. He decid-ed to focus and become a great student, and at that moment he made a goal to attend the University of Georgia. As a more prepared student, he entered his new college with a fresh perspective of studying his hardest and making good grades. He entered into a degree for exercise science without a specific idea of where this path would lead him, but he enjoyed the courses. At that time he made another set of goals for himself: to be a college athlete, receive an athletic scholarship, and to receive a special designation that displays his accom-plishment- called a Letter. As an ath-lete all throughout his younger years, Chris missed competitive athletics and wanted to pursue this new lev-el of competition in college. He accomplished his goal and made the UGA cheerleading team. How did Chris reach this goal? He stated his goal, put it on pa-per, and figured out all the steps to accomplish it.

THINK BIG

What goals do you currently have set? Do you know what steps are needed to accomplish those goals?

Upon graduating from college, Chris's first job was as a cheerleading and tumbling coach at a gym. This was a perfect first job out of college for him, as he always enjoyed athletics, and coaching and training others were natural talents and passions for Chris. After being a coach at a gym for a couple years, he was ready to enter the corporate business world. As a graduate with a degree in exercise science, Chris was concerned that he didn't have the business knowledge and experience many jobs required. A friend mentioned to him that some businesses have corporate training programs that would allow Chris to learn on the job. For the next few years Chris progressed through various **corporations** and learned what skills are needed in the business world. He learned about how to manage people, **delegate** to others, and successfully encourage others to get work done. Chris really enjoyed the aspects of leadership development, which means that successful leaders have skills to encourage others to accomplish tasks and inspire them to reach for bigger and better goals.

THINK BIG

Teamwork as a student or as an employee is a very important skill to have. How can you be a positive team member?

During this time, within his roles of leadership development, Chris made another new goal: to go back to college to get his master's degree in business administration. Remember that as a young student, Chris had no interest in school and academics, so this was another example of Chris not letting his past feelings (of not being smart enough) define the future that he wanted for himself. Chris completed his master's of business administration at the University of Georgia and furthered his leadership career. Even though he was excelling in many aspects of his career, Chris felt like he was tied to his phone and always on-call. He realized that a change was needed. At this same time, his family was also becoming more and more involved in a local non-profit organization, Lighthouse Family Retreat, which serves families that have a child with cancer. The organization takes these families on retreats to the beach so that they can enjoy a special vacation together. Chris's family was donating financially and volunteering on these retreats.

While Chris started to think about a new career direction a new opportunity presented itself: Lighthouse was seeking new leadership. Chris took this opportunity to put in an application for this head leadership role. He had known for many years that his ultimate goal was to become a CEO (chief executive officer) of an organization, but it was not a part of his own personal plan for it be a role within a non-profit organization. Chris is often reminded that he may have a goal, but ultimately doors may open for the correct path even when it initially doesn't seem to match *his* plan. This was certainly not the typical organization that Chris had imagined.

In March 2012 Chris become the chief executive officer of Lighthouse Family Retreat. In the role of CEO, Chris is charged with leading a team that is responsible for following through with all of the duties involved in fulfilling Lighthouse's mission and building its brand to be well known by many. Although a non-profit organization is different from a for-profit business, many of their business practices are the same or similar. Chris oversees all sorts of relationships with volunteers who serve the families on the retreats, with churches who partner in programs, and with donors who give and  support financially. Chris is very passionate about **servant leadership,** a big idea that means that if you want to be a great leader you put others needs before your own. As an executive of an organization, that means that Chris "wins" when he puts others first so that they can grow. His

How can you display servant leadership to your those in your class?

greatest joy as a leader is to see people in their sweet spot. When someone has a talent that lines up with their job, they are in their sweet spot, and they can flourish and create an awesome product or results. This ends up being a win for the entire team.

Throughout Chris's journey, one constant theme keeps showing up: Chris has mastered the ability to coach and lead others and to be an example of servant leadership. As a young swim coach it may have been to help a younger swimmer achieve a personal record, but this coaching ability is still present as he walks with **colleagues** through their roles to achieve professional accomplishments.

BRAND SPOTLIGHT:
LIGHTHOUSE FAMILY RETREAT

Lighthouse Family Retreat has been serving families for over 18 years.

Mission: Lighthouse serves families living through childhood cancer by creating environments on a seaside retreat where families can rest, reconnect, experience joy and find hope in God.

Vision: To serve EVERY family that applies for a Lighthouse Family Retreat.

This year they will provide 18 retreats and serve 210 families. There will be over 2,000 volunteers to serve on the retreats in one year. Since starting the organization, they have served over 2,000 families.

For more information, please visit:
www.lighthousefamilyretreat.org.

YOUR THOUGHTS AND IDEAS AFTER READING CHRIS'S STORY

CONCLUSION

7 Mindsets

The leaders featured in the stories in this first install-ment of the Navigator Series all experienced some characteristics that demonstrate self-empow-erment. This means that they made a choice to choose happiness and see the positive. Nothing necessarily comes "easy" in life, but what is easy is how you interpret the situation.

The 7 Mindsets is an organization that cre-ates programs and content for students and teachers across the nation. Their goal is to share that the basis of their research proves that there are seven ideas that contribute to the thinking that your true happiness and ful-fillment comes from how you choose to see every situation. The five leaders in this book perfectly display these 7 Mindsets. Let's review these ideas and how our leaders displayed them.

1. Everything Is Possible

Dream big, embrace creativity, and expect results.

Dana Spinola, fab'rik

Dana knew at an early age that she *loved* fashion. She more than loved fashion, actually; her heart was bursting with love and a passion for fashion. Dana knew that she wanted fashion to be a part of

her life forever, but she didn't necessarily know *how* it could be a job. Over time, she figured out how she could make it a career in the industry—and then share that dream with other business leaders as well.

Daniel Mason Jones, Muse Salon and Spa

The dream of creativity was always a part of Daniel's life, even though the specifics of his dream were not always clear when he was young. He dreamed of a life full of adventure, excitement, and creativity, and he has certainly accomplished that goal.

2. Passion First

Pursue your authentic talents and deepest interests.

Chris Woodruff, Lighthouse Family Retreat

A constant in Chris's story is his passion to coach and lead others. As a student he was a swim coach, as a college graduate he was a gymnastics coach, and as a professional executive he is constantly coaching and leading others to find their own accomplishment of goals.

Steven Carse, King of Pops

Steven's passion came as a result of starting his business. A passion doesn't always have to be the same when you are 30 as it is when you're 9. Steven has found a tremendous passion regarding the sustainability movement. He is very interested in creating produce for his business that is grown in a meaningful way and wants the waste from his business managed in a substantial way. He desires to be a steward of the land and make all of nature that he touches better off after he leaves.

3. We Are Connected

Explore the synergies in all relationships and learn to empower one another.

Daniel Mason Jones, Muse Salon and Spa

Whom you meet along your journey is so important to your growth and future success. Daniel's parents were always supportive and encouraging. As a young person he enjoyed learning from all of the adults around him. As a student he embraced the ability to learn from his teachers, and as a professional he loves each and every encounter with people around him. He feels so strongly that all relationships with others are stepping-stones to further growth and a learning opportunity. He now uses this mindset to be a mentor to thousands of professionals in the salon industry. Daniel knows he has learned so much along the way and is eager to share that with others.

Arpana Satyu-Burge, Dutch Monkey Doughnuts

There are all types of important relationships in life. Some are good, and some are not so great. We are able to learn and grow from any and all types of relationships. Arpana was able to learn how to be a successful leader from many of her bosses when she was a young pastry chef. Some taught her that when you give back to those who you work with, the best results can come from those relationships. She also experienced negative relationships. (Remember the chef who stole her cookbook? That was an easy lesson on how to not treat people.) The lesson here is that you are much more likely to have amazing results when you are a positive leader.

4. 100% Accountable

Choose to be responsible for your own happiness and success.

Arpana Satyu-Burge, Dutch Monkey Doughnuts

Challenges will come from all situations in life. The important thing to remember is that it depends on how you look at it. When Arpana was diagnosed as an adult with bipolar disorder, she chose to see the positive in the situation and realize that this diagnosis was like receiving a map. Her story will have curves and bends, but now she knows how to navigate the path.

Chris Woodruff, Lighthouse Family Retreats

Do you remember how one summer job made Chris realize that his choices were directing his future path? After working at a factory one summer, he realized he did not want his life to continue in that direction. He made a focused and determined choice to take control of his future choices, and he made some drastic changes about how he looked at his education.

5. Attitude of Gratitude

Seek positives from every experience and be thankful for all you have.

Steven Carse, King of Pops

At the end of the day, Steven is simply grateful for all that he has experienced. He has chosen to see the blessing that his business has had on him, his employees, and his customers. The ability to find gratitude in any and all situations allows Steven to enjoy all that comes his way.

Arpana Satyu-Burge, Dutch Monkey Doughnuts

Arpana's business has seen tremendous success—so much so that she constantly hears suggestions for growing and ex-panding the business. Although this idea might be incredibly appealing to many, Arpana's perspective is gratitude that her business has allowed her to work with her husband, be with her family more, and lead and in-spire others the way that she chooses. She is grateful for its current state and does not see a need to "mess with perfection."

6. Live to Give

Inspire and serve others while maximizing your potential.

Dana Spinola, fab'rik

So many businesses associate with a foundation or charity, but not many businesses create their own. That is just what Dana has done. Not only does she want to use her passion for fashion to give to others, but she wants a front-row seat in the choice to be generous and give to others. She finds that the most rewarding gift for others is the ability to express their inner beauty on the outside even when life challenges pre-vent their capability to shop. Her foundation, Free Fab'rik, has changed the life for so many women, and Dana is ready to see growth in the gift of giving.

Chris Woodruff, Lighthouse Family Retreat

One would assume that the CEO of a charitable organization would be inspired to give to others. Chris takes that mindset to heart as he serves both the retreat families and his employees. Remember discussing servant leadership? Chris's story has consistently displayed this choice that when you give back to those around you, everyone involved wins.

7. The Time Is Now

Harness the power of this moment, and take purposeful action today.

Daniel Mason Jones, Muse Salon and Spa

Daniel went to college with a solid dream. Remember his dream of becoming a funeral director? When he discovered a new passion that would change the direction of his whole future, he knew that he had to harness the power of the moment and change his plan. He displayed purposeful action in taking the needed steps to re-direct his path. Of course, this isn't what he originally planned, but the ability to combine flexibility and determination allowed for Daniel to achieve his final dream of becoming a successful hair stylist.

Dana Spinola, fab'rik

A quote that Dana chooses to follow is "Goals are dreams with a deadline." That perfectly embodies the mindset of purposeful action. As a leader, Dana has led her employees to follow this mindset with a tangible product: She gave all of her employees a five-piece bracelet that matches the five new goals for the business. The bracelets are a visual and tactile reminder of goals and the reason why they created those goals. Purposeful action looks different for all leaders, and for some it can come in the form of a stylish bracelet.

We encourage all of our readers to explore the 7 Mindsets and to see how these ideas can be implemented in your life and at your local school. Visit http://7mindsets.com to learn more.

GLOSSARY

Advisory Board: A group of people gathered together to offer advice to a business or organization.

Budget: An estimate of income (what funds are coming in) and expenses (what funds are being spent) for a given period of time.

Business Plan: A document that defines the business goals and how they are going to accomplish them.

Colleague: A person that one works with.

Community: A group of people living in the same place or having a particular characteristic in common.

Competitor: A person or organization that is doing the same as you and you are trying to establish higher rank.

Corporation: A company or business.

Data: Facts and information that are collected together.

Delegate: The ability to task another person with a responsibility.

Economy: The wealth and resources for our country. This is the cycle of goods and services being produced and the ability for people to purchase them.

Entrepreneurship: The activity of building, organizing, and managing a business.

Financially Responsible: The wise use of money and understanding what income and expenses you have to work with.

Franchise: An agreement in which one established business allows others to use their business model and duplicate the original business as their own.

Internship: A position that a student takes within an organization to gain work experience.

Loan: A sum of money that is borrowed and expected to be paid back.

Servant Leadership: The desire to help those around you and identify their needs so that the group as the whole benefits from accomplished individuals.

Study Skills: Various methods of learning that allow a student to become a long-term and successful learner.

Vendors: A person or company offering something for sale.

Visualize: To form a mental image.

About the Author

Amber Pert has carried many titles along her professional journey: finance manager, business founder, and now writer. But the title she is most proud of is *mom*. As the mom to three young readers, she knows the value of reading to curious minds and the wonderful questions and conversations that are sparked from reading.

Through the founding of her business, The Wellspring Crew, Amber is deeply passionate about sharing business ideas with young readers through the lens of storytelling. Everyone has a story!

Amber and The Wellspring Crew invite you to follow along on our journey as we set out to bring these stories to life. We would also love to hear from you about your stories of what you are building and how you are dreaming big.

Facebook: www.facebook.com/wellspringcrew

Instagram: www.instagram.com/amber_wellspringcrew

Website: www.wellspringcrew.com

Email: hello@wellspringcrew.com

Parents and educators, we invite you to visit our website for free supplementary tools for you to use with your young readers.

Made in the USA
Lexington, KY
03 September 2018